THE BIG PRINT

Copyright 2025

All rights reserved.

This book is protected under copyright law. No part of this publication may be copied, reproduced, stored, or transmitted in any form—electronic, mechanical, photocopying, recording, or otherwise—without prior written permission from the author, except for brief quotations in reviews or articles.

Legal Disclaimer

This book is intended for informational and educational purposes only. It does not substitute professional advice in legal, medical, financial, or psychological matters. The author and publisher disclaim any liability arising from the use or misuse of this content.

Chapter 1: Understanding The Big Print

- **Section 1.1:** Defining The Big Print: What It Means in Your Life
- **Section 1.2:** The Importance of Perspective and Purpose
- **Section 1.3:** Aligning Your Goals with The Big Print

Chapter 2: Seeing the Big Picture

- **Section 2.1:** Developing a Holistic View of Your Life
- **Section 2.2:** Identifying Key Areas for Growth and Transformation
- **Section 2.3:** Overcoming Small-Minded Thinking and Limitations

Chapter 3: Living Out The Big Print

- **Section 3.1:** Taking Bold Actions that Align with Your Vision
- **Section 3.2:** Staying Grounded in Your Faith and Purpose

- **Section 3.3:** Practicing Patience and Persistence in the Process

Chapter 4: Overcoming Obstacles in The Big Print

- **Section 4.1:** Identifying Common Pitfalls and How to Avoid Them
- **Section 4.2:** Using Faith to Navigate Life's Challenges
- **Section 4.3:** Cultivating Resilience and Trust Through Hard Times

Chapter 5: Embracing the Journey

- **Section 5.1:** The Beauty of the Process Over the End Goal
- **Section 5.2:** Celebrating Small Wins and Progress
- **Section 5.3:** Reconnecting with The Big Print When You Feel Lost

Chapter 1: Understanding The Big Print

In our daily lives, we are bombarded with a constant flow of information. Every decision we make, from the simplest to the most significant, is influenced by a set of underlying principles and frameworks. These frameworks can be seen as "the big print" of our lives — the overarching themes, values, and guiding forces that shape our choices and direction. Understanding "the big print" is essential for creating a life of purpose, clarity, and intentionality. This chapter delves into the concept of the big print, breaking it down into components that are practical, meaningful, and applicable to personal development. We will explore its definition, significance, and how aligning it with your goals can lead to a more fulfilling existence.

Section 1.1: Defining The Big Print: What It Means in Your Life

The "big print" is a metaphor for the larger themes that shape our lives. Much like the fine print in a contract that often goes unnoticed but holds the most important details, the big print represents the overarching truths and values that govern our decisions. While the fine print can often be overlooked or ignored, the big print cannot be bypassed if we want to live a life of true meaning and purpose. It includes everything from our core beliefs and values to the larger societal and spiritual influences that mold our thinking.

For some, the big print is something they recognize instinctively. For others, it takes a lifetime to fully understand and internalize. The big print can be defined as:

1. **Your Core Beliefs**: What do you truly believe in at the core of your being? These beliefs may relate to spirituality, relationships, self-worth, and the meaning of life. If you're unsure of what you believe, take a step back and ask yourself what gives you peace or a sense of purpose. The big print begins with these foundational ideas.
2. **The External Forces That Shape You**: Family, culture, society, religion, and experiences influence how we perceive the world and make decisions. These influences can sometimes be seen as the "lens" through which we view life, and they often create the foundation for what the big print means in your life.

3. **The Future Vision**: The big print also encompasses the idea of where you see yourself in the future. It's the long-term vision, whether it's connected to career, relationships, personal growth, or a deeper sense of fulfillment.

For example, let's say you want to build a career. The big print here would not only be your specific career goals, but also the values that drive your ambition, the lessons you've learned from your upbringing, and the long-term purpose behind your work. For instance, if you believe your career is about making an impact, contributing to society, or helping others, that is part of your big print. It guides your decisions, behaviors, and actions every day, whether consciously or subconsciously.

Section 1.2: The Importance of Perspective and Purpose

Having a clear understanding of the big print in your life helps provide the much-needed perspective and purpose to navigate life's challenges and uncertainties. Without this awareness, it's easy to get caught up in the trivialities of everyday life and lose sight of the larger picture.

Perspective is a mental attitude or outlook on life. It's the way we interpret events and the meaning we assign to them. Perspective shapes the way we react to setbacks, opportunities, relationships, and even successes. If we don't have a strong sense of perspective, we may find ourselves bogged down by frustration, confusion, or stress. Without a clear understanding of the big print, the distractions of life can cloud our judgment, leading to feelings of being overwhelmed or lost.

Purpose, on the other hand, is the driving force that keeps us moving forward even in the face of challenges. A sense of purpose helps us stay committed to our goals and navigate difficult times with resilience and determination. When we align our actions with a sense of greater purpose — one that reflects our values, beliefs, and aspirations — we experience a deeper sense of fulfillment. Life becomes more than just about surviving; it becomes about thriving in alignment with our true self.

Together, perspective and purpose provide the internal compass that guides us through life. They help us see beyond the immediate obstacles and setbacks, and focus on the bigger picture. When we understand what the big print means in our lives, we are able to:

- **Make better decisions**: With a clear sense of purpose and perspective, decision-making becomes easier. We can ask ourselves, "Does this align with my core values and long-term goals?" This alignment ensures that we are always moving in the right direction, even when the path seems unclear.
- **Stay focused**: Life is full of distractions. Without the big print guiding our decisions, it's easy to lose focus and drift off course. When we know what truly matters to us, we are more likely to stay focused on our objectives.
- **Embrace challenges**: When life presents difficulties, a strong sense of purpose can help us see them as opportunities for growth. With perspective, we can view challenges as temporary setbacks that will ultimately contribute to our personal development.

Consider the example of someone who is pursuing a career in medicine. Their purpose might be to help others heal, alleviate suffering, and make a tangible impact on society.

In moments of exhaustion, failure, or frustration, that bigger picture keeps them going. They don't lose sight of the importance of their work because they have a clear understanding of their purpose and the role it plays in the greater story of their life.

Section 1.3: Aligning Your Goals with The Big Print

Once you have a clear understanding of the big print in your life — your core beliefs, values, and long-term vision — it's time to ensure that your goals align with it. Without this alignment, you risk pursuing goals that, while perhaps appealing in the short term, may not lead to the fulfillment and satisfaction you truly desire. True success is not just about achieving goals; it's about achieving the right goals — those that resonate with your authentic self.

To align your goals with the big print, consider the following steps:

1. **Clarify Your Values**: What are the core values that define you? These may include integrity, compassion, innovation, family, spirituality, or

community. Once you've identified your values, ask yourself how they can be reflected in your goals. For instance, if compassion is a key value for you, a goal to become a volunteer or engage in charitable work would naturally align with your big print.

2. **Set Long-Term and Short-Term Goals**: While long-term goals help you focus on your vision for the future, short-term goals serve as the actionable steps toward realizing that vision. A clear understanding of the big print can help you prioritize your goals, ensuring that they are stepping stones to the larger purpose.

3. **Evaluate Your Current Goals**: Take a moment to evaluate your existing goals. Are they aligned with your values and purpose? Are you pursuing them because they reflect your true desires, or because of external pressures or expectations? If your goals are out of alignment with your big print, it's important to reassess and recalibrate them.

4. **Be Open to Change**: As you grow and evolve, so too may your big print. Be open to the possibility that your goals might shift as your understanding of your purpose deepens. Life is dynamic, and your goals should reflect that fluidity. Reevaluate your

goals periodically to ensure they continue to align with your evolving perspective.

5. **Take Action**: Ultimately, aligning your goals with your big print is not just a mental exercise. It requires action. Make deliberate steps toward your goals every day, and stay committed to your purpose. Even when things get tough, remember that each action you take brings you closer to living a life that reflects your true self.

For example, if you have a vision of leading a successful business, your goals might include growing your company, cultivating leadership skills, and building strong relationships with employees and clients. However, if you value community and service, you might also set goals around corporate social responsibility or creating a work environment that prioritizes employee well-being.

Conclusion: The Power of the Big Print

Understanding the big print is not just about conceptualizing the grand themes of your life. It's about transforming those ideas into actionable steps and aligning your goals with the greater purpose you wish to fulfill. By defining the big print, embracing perspective and purpose, and ensuring your goals reflect the true essence of who you are, you unlock the potential for a life that is meaningful, fulfilling, and aligned with your deepest values. As you move forward, remember that the big print is not just a destination, but a journey — one that requires patience, reflection, and intentional action.

Chapter 2: Seeing the Big Picture

In life, it is often easy to get caught up in the details of the moment—the day-to-day struggles, challenges, and small victories. While these individual moments are important, they can sometimes distract us from the larger narrative of our lives. Chapter 2 invites us to step back, observe, and understand the bigger picture. It asks us to see beyond the immediate, to develop a holistic perspective, and to identify the key areas of our lives that are ripe for growth and transformation. By doing so, we can become more aware of where we are headed and how we can design our lives in a way that aligns with our true purpose and calling.

Section 2.1: Developing a Holistic View of Your Life

To develop a holistic view of your life means to take into consideration all aspects of your being—emotional, mental, physical, and spiritual—and how they intersect and influence each other. A holistic perspective helps you see yourself not as isolated parts, but as an interconnected whole. This broader view enables you to recognize how different facets of your life are contributing to your overall sense of well-being and fulfillment.

In a world that often encourages compartmentalization, it can be difficult to avoid the temptation to focus solely on one area of life, such as career or personal relationships. While these areas are important, they do not exist in a vacuum. In fact, the way you approach one area has the potential to influence all other aspects of your life. For example, stress in your work life can negatively impact your health and relationships, while poor physical health can affect your ability to think clearly and pursue your dreams. Therefore, developing a holistic view of your life is essential to understanding how to create lasting change and growth.

Understanding the interconnectedness of life is crucial to cultivating this perspective. You cannot focus solely on one area—such as your career or personal development—while ignoring other dimensions, such as your physical health, relationships, or spiritual well-being. They all play an integral role in shaping the person you are and how you move through the world. The key is recognizing that your growth is not just about excelling in one area, but about nurturing a balanced, well-rounded existence that reflects who you are at your core.

One way to begin developing this holistic view is by regularly checking in with yourself. Consider how you are doing across different areas of your life, and be honest about where you are thriving and where you are struggling. Some helpful areas to assess include:

- **Physical health**: Are you taking care of your body? Are you eating well, exercising, and getting adequate sleep?

- **Mental health**: Are you nurturing your emotional well-being? Are you managing stress effectively, and seeking support when needed?
- **Relationships**: Are you fostering meaningful, healthy connections with others? Are you making time for family, friends, and loved ones?
- **Spiritual well-being**: Are you nurturing your connection with your faith or spirituality? Are you practicing self-compassion, forgiveness, and gratitude?
- **Career/Work**: Are you pursuing work that aligns with your passions and purpose? Do you feel fulfilled and challenged in your career?

By regularly evaluating yourself in these areas, you can gain a clearer picture of how each part of your life is influencing the whole. This will help you to identify areas that may need more attention and will provide insight into where you can begin to focus your energy and efforts.

Section 2.2: Identifying Key Areas for Growth and Transformation

Once you develop a holistic view of your life, the next step is identifying the areas that need growth and transformation. It is essential to realize that no one's life is static; we are constantly evolving. The areas where we need growth may vary over time, depending on life circumstances and personal goals, but identifying these areas allows us to take intentional action toward becoming the person we want to be.

To identify key areas for growth, it's helpful to reflect on your values, passions, and goals. What matters most to you? What areas of your life do you feel are holding you back? Often, growth occurs when we push ourselves outside of our comfort zones and make changes in areas that feel stagnant or neglected.

Here are some steps to guide you in identifying these key areas for growth:

1. **Reflect on your current situation**: Take a moment to reflect on where you currently are in your life. What parts of your life feel fulfilling? What parts feel lacking or disconnected? Write down the answers to these questions and look for common themes that could reveal areas where growth is needed.

2. **Clarify your values**: What do you value most in life? Whether it's family, health, career, or personal growth, your values serve as a compass for identifying the areas where you may need to focus. If your career is important to you, but you're feeling disconnected from your work, it may be time to explore how you can align your career with your core values.
3. **Identify your goals**: Consider where you want to be in the next 1-3 years. What steps will you need to take to get there? Break your goals down into smaller, manageable chunks, and identify the areas where you can take immediate action to make progress.
4. **Notice patterns and areas of resistance**: Sometimes, areas that need growth are those where we feel the most resistance or frustration. It could be a relationship that needs mending, a habit you've been meaning to change, or a belief system that's holding you back. Pay attention to these areas and consider how you can move through resistance to make lasting change.
5. **Seek feedback**: Sometimes, we can't see the full picture ourselves. Don't be afraid to ask trusted

friends, family members, or mentors for feedback. They may notice areas in your life that are in need of growth and can offer guidance or perspective.

Once you've identified the areas where you want to grow, break them down into manageable goals. Focus on one or two key areas at a time, and begin taking small steps toward transformation. Change doesn't happen overnight, but by committing to continuous growth, you'll begin to experience meaningful progress in your life.

Section 2.3: Overcoming Small-Minded Thinking and Limitations

One of the greatest barriers to seeing the big picture and embracing growth is small-minded thinking. Small-minded thinking limits our possibilities and keeps us stuck in a narrow view of what we can achieve. It often manifests as self-doubt, fear, or negative beliefs that we have about our capabilities. Overcoming this kind of thinking is essential to breaking free from self-imposed limitations and stepping into a life of greater possibility and fulfillment.

Small-minded thinking often arises from fear—fear of failure, fear of change, and fear of the unknown. When we allow fear to dictate our actions, we may remain in situations that no longer serve us, whether it's staying in a job that drains us, remaining in a toxic relationship, or not taking the risks necessary for growth. In many cases, these fears are rooted in limiting beliefs that have been ingrained in us over time, often based on past experiences or societal conditioning.

The first step in overcoming small-minded thinking is recognizing when it's happening. Are you telling yourself that you're not good enough or capable enough to achieve your goals? Are you allowing fear to dictate your decisions and hold you back from taking bold steps forward?

To break free from this mindset, consider the following strategies:

1. **Challenge your limiting beliefs**: Identify the beliefs that are holding you back, and question their validity. Are they based on facts, or are they rooted in fear or past experiences? Often, limiting beliefs are simply stories we tell ourselves that no longer serve us. By challenging these beliefs, you can reframe your thinking and open up new possibilities for growth.

2. **Practice self-compassion**: Small-minded thinking often arises from a lack of self-compassion. When you're overly critical of yourself, you may become paralyzed by fear of failure or rejection. Practice speaking to yourself with kindness and understanding, just as you would to a friend who was struggling.

3. **Surround yourself with positive influences**: The people you surround yourself with can either reinforce or challenge your small-minded thinking. Seek out individuals who encourage you to dream big, take risks, and think beyond your current circumstances. Positive relationships can help you stay motivated and inspired, even in the face of challenges.

4. **Focus on possibilities, not limitations**: Instead of focusing on what you cannot do, focus on what is possible. Begin to see challenges as opportunities for growth and learning, rather than obstacles to be avoided. This shift in perspective will help you embrace new opportunities and overcome fear-based thinking.

5. **Take action**: The best way to overcome small-minded thinking is through action. When you step

outside your comfort zone and take bold, purposeful steps toward your goals, you'll begin to build confidence and momentum. Taking action, even if it's small at first, is the key to breaking free from the limitations of fear and self-doubt.

By overcoming small-minded thinking, you open the door to greater possibilities and transform your approach to life. You begin to see challenges as stepping stones, rather than roadblocks, and embrace a mindset of abundance and growth.

Seeing the big picture involves cultivating a holistic view of your life, identifying areas for growth, and overcoming small-minded thinking. When you take the time to step back and evaluate where you are, you can gain clarity and direction, empowering you to create lasting change. By developing a mindset of possibility, embracing growth, and pushing through limitations, you can design a life that reflects your deepest values and aspirations.

Chapter 3: Living Out The Big Print

Section 3.1: Taking Bold Actions that Align with Your Vision

Living out the big print of your life requires more than just envisioning a grand future; it calls for bold, decisive action in the present. This section explores the importance of stepping forward in faith, courage, and strategic choices that align with your God-given vision.

Boldness Requires Clarity

Before you can take bold actions, you must first gain clarity on your vision. A vision is not just a goal or a dream; it's a divine picture of where God is leading you. It's a snapshot of the purpose and destiny that He has designed for you to walk into. When the vision is clear, boldness becomes a natural response. It is rooted in a deep confidence in God's calling and the knowledge that He will equip you for the journey.

But how does one cultivate this clarity? It starts with intentional prayer and reflection. Spend time in God's presence, asking for discernment. Look to Scripture, allowing the Holy Spirit to speak to your heart about your unique purpose. Seek counsel from wise mentors who can help refine your understanding of your calling. Clarity is the foundation for all future actions, and without it, you risk walking aimlessly or following the wrong path.

The Power of Bold Choices

Taking bold actions is often more than simply choosing to step out; it's about making choices that align with your vision, even when the circumstances don't feel ideal. Bold choices are those that require a level of trust that goes beyond human understanding. These choices involve risks, challenges, and sometimes, stepping into unknown territory. However, it is in these moments of faith-driven risk that God's provision and guidance become most evident.

Consider the story of Peter walking on the water. He didn't step out onto the waves because the storm had ceased; he stepped out because Jesus called him to. Similarly, you may find that your path to living out the big print is full of obstacles and uncertainty, but the boldness comes when you respond to the call, trusting that God will guide you through the rough waters.

Bold actions may look different for everyone, but they share a common thread: they are in direct alignment with the vision and purpose God has placed on your life. For some, boldness may mean starting a new business, speaking out on an issue that matters, or serving in a ministry that stretches you. For others, it could mean making difficult personal decisions or reaching out to someone in need. The key is that your actions reflect your commitment to the vision, no matter how uncomfortable or uncertain the journey might feel.

Overcoming Fear and Doubt

Fear and doubt are natural when stepping into bold actions. The enemy often uses these emotions to paralyze us and keep us from pursuing God's plan. However, it is crucial to remember that God has not given us a spirit of fear, but of power, love, and a sound mind (2 Timothy 1:7). To overcome fear, focus on the truth of who God is and what He has called you to do.

Start by acknowledging your fear but choose to act despite it. Just like when David faced Goliath, the battle wasn't about the size of the giant but the size of God in comparison. When you fix your eyes on God's ability to lead you through, the fear loses its grip. Bold actions are not the absence of fear; they are the willingness to move forward despite fear.

Section 3.2: Staying Grounded in Your Faith and Purpose

As you take bold actions, it's important to remain grounded in your faith and purpose. In a world that constantly pulls our attention in different directions, it can be easy to lose sight of why we're doing what we're doing. This section emphasizes the importance of staying rooted in faith, keeping your purpose in focus, and remaining anchored in God's Word as you navigate your journey.

Faith as Your Anchor

Faith is not just a feeling or a momentary belief; it's the bedrock that supports your actions, thoughts, and decisions. It is your unwavering confidence in God's goodness and His plan for your life. Without faith, bold actions can quickly turn into reckless decisions or moves driven by personal ambition rather than divine direction.

Staying grounded in faith means continually cultivating a trust in God's promises. It means regularly spending time in prayer, worship, and the Word. You must remind yourself daily that your purpose is not based on your own abilities but on God's power working within you. Faith allows you to step out confidently, knowing that God will guide you in every decision.

One powerful way to stay grounded in faith is through regular scripture meditation. Find verses that speak to your purpose and vision. For example, Jeremiah 29:11 reminds us, "For I know the plans I have for you," declares the Lord, "plans to prosper you and not to harm you, plans to give you a hope and a future." By reflecting on these truths, you solidify your trust that God is faithful to His Word.

Purpose as Your Compass

Your purpose serves as the compass that keeps you aligned with God's will. When you know your purpose, you can filter every decision, relationship, and action through it. Purpose is not a vague idea but a specific calling that God has placed on your life. It's the unique contribution you are meant to make in this world, through your talents, experiences, and passions.

The key to staying grounded in your purpose is consistency. Regularly revisit the "big print" vision that God has placed before you. Reflect on how each action you take fits into this larger picture. Staying connected to your purpose keeps you focused, preventing distractions from pulling you away from the path God has laid out for you.

When challenges arise, remember that your purpose is greater than the momentary hardships. It's easy to become discouraged or distracted when facing adversity, but staying anchored in your purpose helps you persevere. Just as Jesus remained focused on the joy set before Him, we too can press forward knowing that our lives are aligned with a greater mission.

Community as Your Strength

Staying grounded in faith and purpose also requires surrounding yourself with like-minded individuals who can encourage, support, and hold you accountable. Community is vital for spiritual growth and direction. Find people who share your values, who can pray with you, and who can offer godly wisdom when you face challenges.

Proverbs 27:17 says, "As iron sharpens iron, so one person sharpens another." The right community helps you stay grounded by providing perspective, encouragement, and accountability. When the path gets tough, lean on those around you to remind you of your calling and the faithfulness of God.

Section 3.3: Practicing Patience and Persistence in the Process

In the pursuit of your vision, there will be times when things don't happen as quickly as you expect or when progress seems slow. This section delves into the importance of practicing patience and persistence, understanding that the process is often as significant as the outcome.

The Waiting Period

In the Kingdom of God, waiting is not a passive state but an active process of trusting and preparing. It is in the waiting that our character is refined, our faith is strengthened, and our trust in God deepens. Think of the story of Abraham. God gave him a promise, but it took years for that promise to come to fruition. During that time,

Abraham had to trust God's timing, even when circumstances seemed to contradict what God had said.

When waiting feels difficult, remember that God's timing is perfect. What may seem like a delay is often God's way of preparing you for something greater. Patience in the process is a sign of maturity and trust. Instead of rushing ahead, take time to learn, grow, and build the foundation for what God is calling you to do. It is often in the waiting that you develop the qualities needed to sustain success when it comes.

Persistence through the Challenges

Persistence is the ability to continue moving forward, even when faced with obstacles. Living out your purpose often requires facing setbacks, challenges, and discouragement. It's easy to give up when things get tough, but persistence is what keeps you on track. The Apostle Paul famously said, "Let us not become weary in doing good, for at the proper time we will reap a harvest if we do not give up" (Galatians 6:9).

Persisting through difficult times means maintaining a mindset of endurance. It involves seeing the process as part of your growth rather than something to endure for the sake of an end result. Keep in mind that God's power is made perfect in our weakness (2 Corinthians 12:9). The challenges you face are opportunities for God to show Himself strong in your life.

Trusting the Process

Ultimately, patience and persistence are both rooted in trust—trust that God is working in and through you, even when the results aren't immediately visible. Trusting the process means believing that God is using every step, every challenge, and every delay to shape you into the person you need to be in order to fulfill your calling.

In summary, living out the big print involves more than just vision; it requires bold actions, grounded faith, and a willingness to wait and persist through the process. Trust in God's timing, stay aligned with your purpose, and practice patience as you move forward in the journey.

Chapter 4: Overcoming Obstacles in The Big Print

Obstacles are an inevitable part of life. Whether it is a personal challenge, a professional setback, or an emotional trial, each individual faces difficulties that test their endurance, faith, and character. But how we approach these obstacles makes all the difference. Overcoming them is not about avoiding difficulty but developing the right tools to navigate the storm. This chapter delves into overcoming obstacles by identifying common pitfalls, utilizing faith as a guide, and cultivating resilience and trust during difficult times.

Section 4.1: Identifying Common Pitfalls and How to Avoid Them

In the journey of overcoming obstacles, one of the most powerful steps is awareness. Recognizing the common pitfalls that often derail progress can help prevent us from falling into traps that hinder our growth. These pitfalls come in many forms, and they can range from internal struggles, like self-doubt, to external factors such as distractions or negative influences.

1. **The Pitfall of Self-Doubt**

Self-doubt is one of the most pervasive obstacles that can cripple an individual's ability to move forward. It manifests as a voice of discouragement in your mind, telling you that you're not enough, that you're not capable, or that failure is inevitable. This inner critic often arises in the face of a challenge, trying to convince you to avoid taking risks or to abandon your goals. The key to avoiding this pitfall is recognizing that self-doubt is a natural response, not a reality.

How to Avoid Self-Doubt:

- **Affirmations:** Replace negative thoughts with affirmations. Remind yourself of your past successes and strengths. Acknowledge the skills and talents you possess that have helped you overcome past obstacles.
- **Faith in Your Purpose:** Trust that the challenges you face are part of a bigger plan, and that you have been equipped to handle them. Your purpose and faith in God can serve as powerful motivators.
- **Surround Yourself with Encouragement:** Stay close to people who believe in you, encourage you, and challenge you to grow. A supportive

community can combat self-doubt and help you stay grounded in truth.

2. **The Pitfall of Procrastination**

Procrastination is often a defense mechanism against discomfort or fear. When facing an obstacle, the emotional weight of the challenge can cause you to delay taking action, either out of fear of failure or a feeling of overwhelm. Procrastination allows the problem to persist and grow, often making it more difficult to resolve in the future.

How to Avoid Procrastination:

- **Break it Down:** One of the most effective ways to overcome procrastination is to break the task or challenge into smaller, manageable steps. This reduces the overwhelming feeling and makes it easier to begin.
- **Set Time Limits:** Commit to dedicating a set amount of time to the task. Knowing that there is a specific time frame can motivate you to start and keep you focused.

- **Accountability:** Share your goals with someone you trust, and allow them to hold you accountable. The pressure of knowing that someone is following up on your progress can push you to act.

3. **The Pitfall of External Negative Influences**

The world around you can be filled with negative influences that try to deter you from moving forward. Whether it's toxic relationships, discouraging comments from others, or societal pressures, these external factors can play a significant role in obstructing your path.

How to Avoid External Negative Influences:

- **Limit Exposure:** Protect yourself from negativity by limiting your exposure to toxic people or environments. Sometimes, distancing yourself from sources of discouragement is the best way to regain clarity and focus.
- **Set Boundaries:** Set clear boundaries to protect your emotional health. It's okay to say no to requests or situations that drain you or distract you from your goals.

- **Stay True to Your Values:** Remember your core values and beliefs. Let them serve as a compass, guiding you through external pressures. When you have clarity about your values, it's easier to stay focused and unaffected by outside distractions.

4. **The Pitfall of Lack of Preparation**

Many obstacles arise because we aren't fully prepared to face them. Whether we haven't planned for a possible challenge or haven't acquired the necessary skills or knowledge, a lack of preparation can make obstacles seem insurmountable.

How to Avoid Lack of Preparation:

- **Continuous Learning:** Embrace a mindset of growth and learning. Equip yourself with the tools, skills, and knowledge necessary to face challenges head-on.
- **Plan Ahead:** Take time to anticipate potential obstacles and plan for them. Having a strategy in place helps you feel confident and capable when challenges arise.

- **Seek Guidance:** Sometimes preparation means seeking wisdom from others. Don't hesitate to ask for advice or guidance from mentors, peers, or those who have walked a similar path.

Section 4.2: Using Faith to Navigate Life's Challenges

Faith is not simply a passive belief; it is an active force that enables us to navigate life's toughest challenges. When faced with difficulties, it's easy to become consumed by fear, anxiety, or frustration. However, by anchoring ourselves in faith—faith in God's goodness, His plan for our lives, and His ability to bring good out of hardship—we can find the strength to persevere.

1. **The Role of Faith in Times of Trial**

Faith is not just for the mountaintop moments; it's in the valleys of struggle that faith has the potential to transform us. The Bible teaches us that we will face trials in this world, but that we are not meant to face them alone. Faith is the trust that God is with us, even in the darkest of times.

Faith in Action:

- **Trust God's Plan:** Even when circumstances seem bleak, trust that God has a plan for you. Romans 8:28 reminds us that "in all things, God works for the good of those who love Him." Our faith gives us the assurance that no challenge is wasted.
- **Prayer:** Engage in regular prayer to deepen your connection with God. Prayer is not just about asking for help; it's about aligning your heart with His will and seeking His strength and wisdom.
- **Scripture as Strength:** God's Word is filled with promises and stories of overcoming adversity. By meditating on Scripture, we can draw strength and encouragement. Scriptures like Philippians 4:13 ("I can do all things through Christ who strengthens me") empower us to face any challenge.

2. **Faith as a Source of Hope and Peace**

When facing obstacles, we can often feel overwhelmed by the weight of our circumstances. Faith acts as an anchor, providing us with hope and peace in the midst of chaos. With faith, we recognize that our present struggles do not define us and that God's peace surpasses understanding.

Faith-Fueled Peace:

- **Let Go of Control:** Faith allows us to surrender control and trust in God's timing. When we stop striving in our own strength and submit to God's will, we can experience His peace.
- **Focus on the Eternal:** Obstacles may feel significant in the moment, but they are temporary in light of eternity. Remembering that God is working for our eternal good helps put trials into perspective.

3. **Faith as a Guide Through Uncertainty**

One of the most challenging aspects of obstacles is the uncertainty they bring. When the outcome is unclear or when the road ahead seems murky, faith provides us with guidance. It is through faith that we can take the next step, even without knowing what lies ahead.

Walking by Faith:

- **One Step at a Time:** Trust God for the next step. You may not have the whole journey mapped out, but faith enables you to trust that each step is part of a greater plan.
- **The Light of His Word:** Psalm 119:105 tells us, "Your word is a lamp to my feet and a light to my

path." When the path ahead is unclear, God's Word illuminates the way, helping us navigate life's challenges.

Section 4.3: Cultivating Resilience and Trust Through Hard Times

Resilience is the ability to bounce back from adversity, to keep moving forward despite obstacles. It's a crucial trait in overcoming challenges, and it's something we can cultivate, especially in times of hardship. Resilience doesn't mean we are immune to pain, but it does mean that we have the strength to withstand it and emerge stronger.

1. **Building Resilience Through Challenges**

The challenges we face in life provide opportunities for growth. While it's natural to wish for an easy path, it's often through hardship that we develop resilience. God uses our struggles to shape our character, refine our faith, and build the perseverance necessary to tackle future challenges.

How to Build Resilience:

- **Adopt a Growth Mindset:** Embrace challenges as opportunities for growth. When we view obstacles as learning experiences rather than roadblocks, we can approach them with confidence and optimism.
- **Learn from Past Experiences:** Reflect on previous hardships and how you overcame them. Recognizing your ability to overcome past challenges can give you the strength to face current obstacles.
- **Stay Committed to Your Goals:** Resilience is nurtured by staying focused on your goals, even when the road gets tough. Commit to moving forward, one step at a time, no matter the setbacks.

2. **Trusting God in the Process**

Trust is the foundation of resilience. Trusting God's sovereignty, His timing, and His ability to work all things for good helps us stay anchored during difficult times. When we trust in God, we recognize that we don't have to control the outcome, and that He is at work in our lives, even when we don't see it.

How to Cultivate Trust:

- **Let Go of Anxiety:** Trust that God is in control. Philippians 4:6-7 encourages us to "do not be anxious about anything, but in every situation, by prayer and petition, with thanksgiving, present your requests to God." Trusting God with our worries allows us to experience His peace.
- **Keep Moving Forward in Faith:** Even when you don't see the way forward, trust God to lead you. Sometimes, trust means taking the next step, even when the future is unclear.

3. **Embracing God's Strength in Weakness**

Resilience is not about relying on our own strength but recognizing that our weakness allows room for God's strength. In 2 Corinthians 12:9, God promises, "My grace is sufficient for you, for my power is made perfect in weakness." Embracing our limitations opens the door for God to work in and through us in powerful ways.

How to Embrace God's Strength:

- **Surrender Control:** Surrender your weakness to God and allow Him to strengthen you. Recognize that in your weakness, He is made strong.

- **Lean on His Grace:** Trust in God's grace to sustain you. When you feel like giving up, remember that His grace is enough to carry you through.

By recognizing common pitfalls, leaning on faith, and cultivating resilience, we can face life's challenges with courage and strength. Obstacles may come, but with God by our side, we can overcome anything.

Chapter 5: Embracing the Journey

In a world that often glorifies the destination, it's easy to forget that the true beauty lies in the journey itself. Too often, we focus on the end goal, the point at which we think everything will finally fall into place. Yet, when we zoom out and examine our lives through a broader lens, we come to realize that it's the journey—how we navigate through challenges, growth, and transformation—that truly defines who we are. In this chapter, we will explore how embracing the journey can lead to more meaningful fulfillment, richer experiences, and a deeper sense of purpose.

Section 5.1: The Beauty of the Process Over the End Goal

The modern world often promotes a "success at all costs" mentality, with the end goal as the ultimate focus. We're taught from a young age that the finish line is where true satisfaction lies—whether it's graduating from school, landing a dream job, achieving a certain weight, or even attaining financial freedom. These goals are valuable, of course, but they often come at the expense of embracing the process, which holds just as much potential for growth and fulfillment.

The problem with fixating on the end goal is that it can overshadow the present moment. Life becomes a race, and we often find ourselves focused on what's next rather than on the process we're currently living through. We might ask ourselves, "When will I be happy?" or "When will I feel accomplished?" But these questions miss the point. True satisfaction doesn't only lie at the end of a long road; it can be found in the journey itself. In fact, it is the journey that shapes us, teaches us, and refines us into the people we are meant to become.

Take, for example, the process of learning a new skill. Whether it's a musical instrument, a foreign language, or a new business venture, the beauty is not just in the final proficiency or success. It's in the small victories along the way—the moments when a new chord finally clicks, when a word in another language feels familiar, or when you make a breakthrough in a project. These moments are as valuable as the end result, because they are the stepping stones to deeper understanding and mastery.

When we embrace the process, we shift our perspective from one of frustration and impatience to one of gratitude and mindfulness. We begin to appreciate the challenges, knowing that they are part of the unfolding journey that is shaping us. The process is what cultivates resilience, patience, and adaptability—qualities that are essential not just for achieving a goal, but for navigating life itself.

Moreover, the process allows us to grow emotionally, mentally, and spiritually in ways that a destination alone cannot. The end goal may give us a moment of satisfaction, but it is the process—the daily practice, the setbacks, the lessons learned—that truly deepens our character and our connection with ourselves and others.

As we move forward in life, it's essential to recognize that the beauty of the journey lies in the experiences we have along the way, not just in the destination. Every step we take—no matter how small—moves us closer to becoming the person we are meant to be. So, instead of focusing solely on the end goal, let us learn to cherish the journey, for it is where the real transformation happens.

Section 5.2: Celebrating Small Wins and Progress

One of the most powerful ways to stay motivated and continue embracing the journey is by celebrating the small wins and progress along the way. In a culture that often focuses on grand accomplishments, it can be easy to overlook the incremental steps that contribute to long-term success. However, these small wins are not just insignificant milestones; they are the building blocks of larger achievements and should be celebrated.

Celebrating small wins helps us shift our focus from perfectionism to progress. Perfectionism can be paralyzing, as it places an unrealistic standard on what success looks like. It demands that we be flawless in our efforts, making it easy to feel discouraged or inadequate when things don't go as planned. But small wins remind us that growth doesn't happen overnight. It's a process—a series of incremental steps that add up over time.

For instance, if you're working on building a healthier lifestyle, the journey might feel long and overwhelming. The ultimate goal might be to lose weight, run a marathon, or feel more energetic. But along the way, there will be many small victories that are just as important. Maybe you completed a week of consistent workouts, or perhaps you made healthier food choices for a few days in a row. These moments are worth celebrating because they represent progress—proof that you're moving in the right direction.

Celebrating small wins also helps us build momentum. When we recognize and acknowledge our progress, it fuels our motivation and strengthens our commitment to the process. It's easy to get discouraged when we focus solely on the end goal, especially when it feels far out of reach. However, when we celebrate the little victories along the way, we start to see that progress is happening, even if it's slower than we would like. This awareness makes the journey feel more rewarding, and it encourages us to keep going.

Small wins also promote a sense of accomplishment and self-worth. In a world that often measures success by big, dramatic achievements, it's easy to forget that progress is still progress, no matter how small. Every positive step you take is a victory—whether it's learning a new skill, making a difficult decision, or overcoming a challenge. These wins build your confidence and reinforce the belief that you are capable of achieving your goals.

To make the most of your small wins, take the time to celebrate them intentionally. This could mean acknowledging your progress through a simple moment of gratitude, treating yourself to something special, or sharing your victories with others. By doing so, you reinforce the idea that the process itself is valuable, and you begin to appreciate how far you've come, not just how far you have to go.

Section 5.3: Reconnecting with The Big Print When You Feel Lost

At times, the journey can feel overwhelming. When obstacles arise, or when progress seems slow, it's easy to lose sight of the bigger picture. We may become consumed by self-doubt, frustration, or confusion, causing us to feel lost or disconnected from our sense of purpose. During these moments, it's important to reconnect with the "big print"—the overarching vision or purpose that initially inspired us to begin the journey.

The "big print" is the larger purpose or vision that gives our lives meaning. It's the reason we set goals in the first place and the vision that guides us through life's challenges. Reconnecting with the big print is essential when we feel lost, as it helps us realign our actions with our deeper values and motivations.

One way to reconnect with the big print is to reflect on why you started your journey in the first place. What was the original inspiration behind your goal? What values are driving your actions? Recalling your deeper "why" helps you remember that your journey is part of a larger story— one that is meaningful and significant.

Another way to reconnect with the big print is through spiritual practices or mindfulness. For those who believe in a higher power, prayer, meditation, or quiet reflection can provide clarity and peace. These practices help us step outside of our current challenges and reconnect with a sense of divine guidance and purpose. In moments of uncertainty, it's essential to remember that the journey is not just about what we achieve, but also about how we grow and how we are shaped by the experiences along the way.

When we reconnect with the big print, we regain perspective. We remind ourselves that the ups and downs of the journey are temporary and that the bigger picture is what truly matters. This shift in perspective helps us navigate challenges with greater resilience and patience, knowing that our struggles are part of a greater narrative.

If you find yourself feeling lost, take a moment to reflect on your journey. Look back at how far you've come, acknowledge the progress you've made, and reconnect with the bigger purpose behind your actions. When you do, you'll find that your path becomes clearer, and your sense of purpose is renewed.

Conclusion

Embracing the journey is an invitation to fully experience life, to recognize that growth, fulfillment, and transformation happen not just at the destination, but in the process itself. By shifting our focus from the end goal to the journey, we can cultivate a deeper sense of gratitude, progress, and purpose. Celebrating small wins along the way helps us stay motivated and committed, while reconnecting with the big print ensures that we stay aligned with our deeper purpose.

The beauty of life lies not in the final destination, but in the way we show up, grow, and embrace each step along the way. As we continue on our respective journeys, let us remember to celebrate the process, cherish the small wins, and stay connected to the bigger picture that gives our lives meaning.

Made in United States
Troutdale, OR
04/19/2025